Measure Up!

AREA, DISTANCE, AND VOLUME

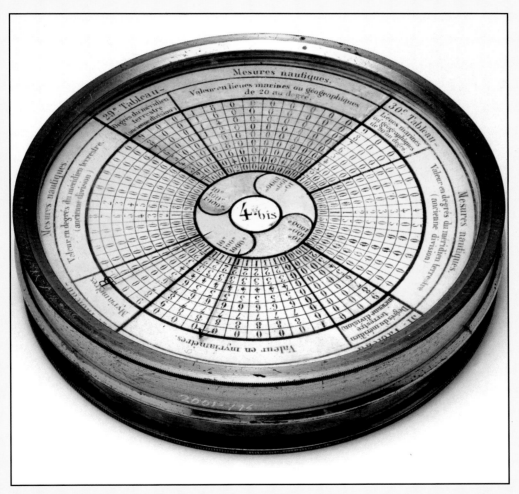

Navin Sullivan

mc Marshall Cavendish
Benchmark
New York

Marshall Cavendish Benchmark
99 White Plains Road
Tarrytown, New York 10591
www.marshallcavendish.us

Library of Congress Cataloging-in-Publication Data

Sullivan, Navin.
  Area, distance, and volume / by Navin Sullivan.
      p. cm. — (Measure up!)
  Summary: "Discusses area, distance, and volume, the science behind measuring area, distance, and volume, and the different devices used to measure them"—Provided by publisher.
  Includes bibliographical references and index.
  ISBN-13: 978-0-7614-2323-2
  ISBN-10: 0-7614-2323-0
  1. Mensuration—Juvenile literature. 2. Metric system—Juvenile literature. I. Title. II. Series.

  QA465.S8 2006
  516'.15--dc22
  2006026394

Editor: Karen Ang
Editorial Director: Michelle Bisson
Art Director: Anahid Hamparian
Series Designer: Alex Ferrari

Photo Research by Iain Morrison

Title page caption: A nineteenth-century metric converter
Cover: Creatas/Superstock

The photographs in this book are used by permission and through the courtesy of: *Alamy:* Bubbles Photolibrary, 15 (right); Brand X Pictures, 21. *Corbis:* David Zimmerman, 18; Kit Kittle, 27; Gregor Schuster/Zefa, 29. *The Image Works:* SSPL, title, 15 (left), 34; Science Museum, London/Topham-HIP, 10; AAAC/Topham, 24; Rachel Epstein, 35. *Art Resource:* Erich Lessing, iv, 6. *Photo Researchers, Inc.:* Andrew Lambert Photography: 13; Simon Fraser, 14; Norm Thomas, 32. *Science Photo Library:* Jon Lomberg, 17. *SuperStock:* 12. *U.S. Department of Commerce:* 8.

Printed in China
1 3 5 6 4 2

Contents

This wallpainting from an Egyptian pharaoh's tomb shows servants using ropes to measure a farm field.

CHAPTER ONE

Customary and Metric Measures

Imagine that you are designing a new house. What would you need to know in order to start your plans? First, you would need to know the **area** of the land you have. Next, you need to plan the layout and size of each room. Based on your plans, the builder would then need to figure out how much material is needed to build your home.

But in order to tell the builder what you need, you would have to use measurements that you both understood. For example, you would not tell the builder that the wood for the house should be about a tree-trunk long. That would puzzle the builder because trees differ in height. And to explain how much land you have to build upon, you would not say, "It takes less than a minute to walk across the yard."

The same was true thousands of years ago. When building pyramids and temples or constructing roads, architects and engineers needed units of length that everyone could understand.

THE HUMAN BODY

The earliest units of measurement were based on the human body. The Ancient Egyptians defined units of length around 5,000 years ago. The thickness of a man's thumb across the base became the inch. A foot was measured from the heel to the tip of the big toe. A yard was equal

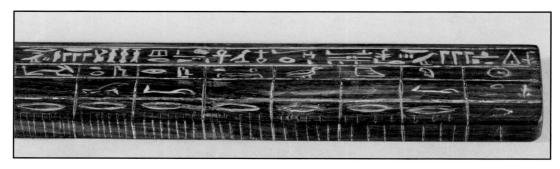

This wooden measuring ruler was used in Ancient Egypt around 332 BCE.

to the distance between the tip of the middle finger of an outstretched arm to a person's nose.

For longer distances, the Ancient Greeks used the **stade.** This measurement was considered to be the length of 100 paces of a marching man. (A pace was the combined length of a stride made with one leg followed by a stride with the other leg.) The stade equaled about 1/10 of our mile, and was used to measure distances in Olympic races. The amphitheater where the races were held was called the stadium.

The Ancient Romans also set distance by the paces of a marching man. They defined a mile as 1,000 paces or 1,620 yards. Sometimes the Roman mile is quoted as 5,000 Roman feet.

Using the human body for measures can cause problems. We all vary in size. A yard for someone with long arms would be different from a yard measured by a person with shorter arms. From one person to another, foot length would also be different. Standard lengths were therefore averaged from the measurements of many individuals. But this created another problem: Lengths from one country or kingdom to another were not the same because the various groups of people were different sizes.

THE METRIC SYSTEM

After the French Revolution, the French invented a new system of units. In 1799, they threw out the old measures of the mile, the yard, and the foot. They developed a new system based not upon the human body, but upon Earth itself. They thought Earth was a better basis of measurement for all mankind.

DEFINING THE METER

The French wanted their new unit of length, the meter, to be exactly 1/40,000,000 of Earth's **circumference.** (A circumference is the distance around a circle or sphere.) But how long was that circumference? In 1792 they appointed two scientists to physically measure part of it.

The two scientists were Jean Baptiste Joseph Delambre and Pierre François André Méchain. Delambre went to Dunkirk, on the north coast of France. Méchain went south to Barcelona, Spain. (These cities are about the same distance apart as Roanoke, Virginia, and New York City.) Astronomers assumed that Delambre and Méchain were separated by 1/36 of Earth's circumference. They figured that if the exact distance between them were measured, they would be able to multiply that by 36 to get the total circumference of the planet. In 1799, they had the exact distance. Now the French could define the meter.

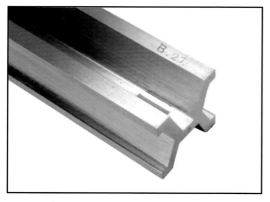

An example of the standard meter bar is kept by the National Institute of Standards and Technology in Maryland.

The standard meter was engraved on a bar made of the metals platinum and iridium. Multiple bars were made and sent to different countries to serve as a standard. Today, however, we do not use a bar to define a meter. The meter is now defined by the distance that light travels in a vacuum (a space with no matter in it) during 1/299,792,458 of a second.

CUSTOMARY MEASUREMENTS

Despite the almost universal acceptance of the metric system, Americans continue to use customary measures. Customary—or traditional—measurements are not based in meters, centimeters, or millimeters. Instead, the system uses inches, feet, yards, and miles. Scientists and engineers in the United States use the metric system so that they can easily exchange information with scientists from other countries. But in schools and in most everyday cases, Americans use the customary system instead of the metric system.

METRIC MIX-UPS

Sometimes having two different systems of measurement can cause problems. For example, in 1999, a Mars space probe was launched with yards instead of meters built into its navigation program. This navigation error caused the spacecraft, the *Mars Climate Orbiter,* to enter the Martian atmosphere, instead of going into orbit above the atmosphere. The orbiter was destroyed by conditions in the planet's atmosphere. This was probably the most expensive mistake between customary and metric units ever made.

UNITS OF LENGTH

Customary	Metric
1 foot = 12 inches	1 micron = 1/1,000 millimeter
1 yard = 3 feet	1 millimeter = 1/1,000 meter
1 mile = 1,760 yards	1 centimeter = 1/100 meter
or 5,280 feet	1 kilometer = 1,000 meters

CUSTOMARY CONVERSIONS

To convert customary units to metric units you can do the following:

To change	into	multiply by
miles	kilometers	1.61
yards	meters	.914
feet	meters	.305
inches	centimeters	2.54

METRIC CONVERSIONS

To convert metric units to customary units you can do the following:

To change	into	multiply by
kilometers	miles	.62
meters	yards	1.09
meters	feet	3.28
centimeters	inches	.39

This 50-foot tape measure from the 1840s was stored in a case that also held a notebook. The handle on the side dispensed and rolled up the tape measure.

CHAPTER TWO

Measuring Tools

Throughout history, different tools have been created to measure length or distance. Once the length of a foot was defined, people needed to be able to refer to it when measuring things. The Egyptians created a tool called a foot rule. This measuring tool became a prized possession. Today foot rules are called rulers. For measurements that are many feet long, it is more helpful to use a longer measuring tool. This is why the yardstick was invented. The yardstick could measure 3 feet at a time since a yard is equal to 3 feet. Similarly, a meter rule or meter stick is used to measure 1 meter.

Tape measures save more time than yardsticks. Some tape measures can even measure up to 100 feet. They

ESTIMATES

Take a ruler and measure across the base of your thumb. How close is it to an actual inch? Using a yardstick, tape measure, or long piece of string, stretch your arm out away from your body and measure from the tip of your middle finger to your nose. How close is this to an actual yard? Have a friend or family member take measurements based on their own fingers and arms. How close are their measurements to an actual inch or yard?

are especially convenient because they are usually compact and easy to carry and use. Tape measures can be made from plastic, metal, or even cloth. The flexibility of the tape measure helps people measure curves or other distances that are not straight lines. For example, a seamstress or tailor uses a cloth tape measure to measure waistlines.

An object's thickness can be measured with a **caliper.** Calipers can be used to measure a variety of objects. Engineers may use calipers to gage the thickness of material such as sheet metal or steel wire. Most versions of the caliper have two jaws or arms controlled by a screw mechanism. The screw mechanism closes the caliper's two arms on the object being measured. When the arms are tight around the object, a distance is displayed on a measuring scale on the caliper. This distance is the object's thickness or width.

Calipers can come in many forms. Sometimes the measurements are shown like marks on a ruler or a dial, or displayed digitally.

A biologist uses a caliper to measure the shell of a tortoise. The measurement is displayed digitally on a screen on the side of the caliper.

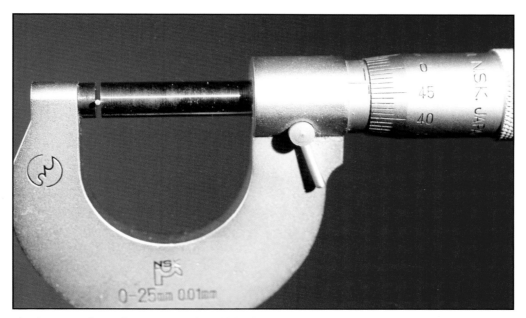

A micrometer is used to measure the width of a very fine piece of wire.

Some calipers do not use a screw mechanism, and instead have one fixed arm and an arm that slides back and forth.

For really thin objects, calipers are not precise enough. Instead, engineers and scientists use a micrometer. This tool has parts that are so thin and small that they can measure something that is 1/1,000 (or .001) millimeter. This measurement—1/1000 millimeter—is also called a micrometer or a micron.

TRIANGULATION

Advances in math and science led to the creation of measuring tools that were easy to use. If a land surveyor from the past had to measure a long distance, he would most likely have to use a measuring stick or chain over and over again to calculate the long distance. Today, land surveyors measure distances by using simple geometry. Using angles, triangles, and the distances between the lengths of the triangles, they are able to measure long distances.

The tools that many surveyors use are a long tape measure or a measuring chain and a theodolite. The measuring tape or chain helps them start their measurements. They use the theodolite to view distances. It is like a little telescope mounted on a platform, usually raised on legs. The theodolite is marked with degrees and other measurements that will help with calculations.

Scientists use a theodolite to help them calculate distances in the frozen Arctic.

PEDOMETERS

A distance-measuring device that has been popular for hundreds of years is the pedometer. You carry or clip on the pedometer as you walk or run, and it will measure the distance that you are traveling. This small instrument senses when your hips move, and then counts the movement as steps. The mechanisms that control pedometers may vary. Some have a spring mechanism that moves up and down as you move. Electronic pedometers use electrical circuits to sense movement. Pedometers are not always accurate in their measurements, but a good-quality device can be pretty close.

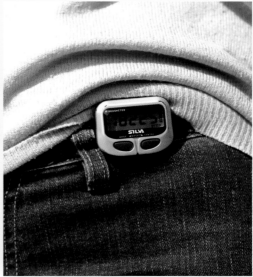

The eighteenth-century pedometer on the left kept track of how it swung as a person walked. Newer pedometers, such as the one shown on the right, count your steps.

PARALLAX

Some early measuring tools were not actual instruments, but were instead concepts or equations. During the second century CE an Egyptian astronomer named Claudius Ptolemy came up with a way of measuring very long distances. It used the concept of **parallax.**

If you look at an object from two different positions, it appears to move against its background. (The easiest way to do this is to focus on an object in front of you, and look at it with one eye closed. Then look at it with the other eye open and the first eye closed. The object seems to move.) The object is not moving, but seems that way because the angles from which you are viewing the object are different. Parallax is the distance that the object appeared to have moved.

Ptolemy used parallax to calculate the distance from Earth to the Moon. For his background, Ptolemy used prominent stars. He recorded the apparent position of the Moon against them. Miles away, an assistant did the same. (Using their two viewpoints was like using one eye, then the other.) Lining up on the two positions, he measured the tiny angle between them.

This tiny angle became part of a very long, narrow triangle. The base of the triangle was the distance (in miles) between their viewpoints. The two long sides were the same length, and each equaled the distance to the Moon. Since Ptolemy knew the baseline measurement and the tiny angle, he used geometric equations to figure out the length of the sides. His result was close to the actual figure of 240,000 miles.

Today, sophisticated technology is used to measure such distances. But these tools were first based on parallax experiments. Astronomers still use parallax when calculating distances between stars.

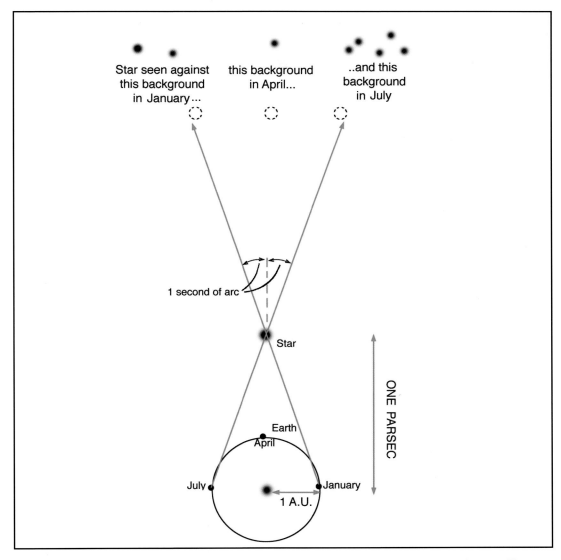

Star seen against this background in January... this background in April... ..and this background in July

1 second of arc

Star

ONE PARSEC

Earth
April

July   January

1 A.U.

This diagram shows how astronomers use parallax to measure the distance of a nearby star. The baseline that they use is the distance between the two positions of Earth at a six-month interval (January and July). Using this baseline of 186,000,000 miles, and the different angles of view at each end, astronomers can calculate the distance to the nearby star.

Horse farms use miles of fencing on their grounds. But in order to know how much they need, the owners of the farm need to calculate the perimeters of their fields.

CHAPTER THREE

Measuring Distance

DISTANCE IN MAPS

Most maps are drawn to scale. This means that the distances between different points on the map correspond to the real distances of the actual locations. For example, a map may use a scale in which 1 inch represents 100 miles. So if the distance between two cities is 300 miles, then the map will space the cities apart by 3 inches.

Sometimes maps have a scale both in miles and kilometers. The size of the scale used depends on how detailed the map is. A map of the United States might have 1 inch representing 150 miles. A map of a single state will show more detail, so the scale might use 1 1/4 inch for 15 miles. A city map might use 7/16 inch for 1 mile. Switching to larger-scale maps is like using a magnifying glass to zoom in.

Sometimes a scale is shown as a ratio. A scale of 1:20 means that each length in the drawing is 1/20 of its actual length. With a map of the world, the scale may be 1:76,000,000!

PERIMETER

Measuring the perimeter means measuring the total length of an object's outside borders. For example, the perimeter of a square, rectangle, or other many-sided shape is the total length of all of its sides.

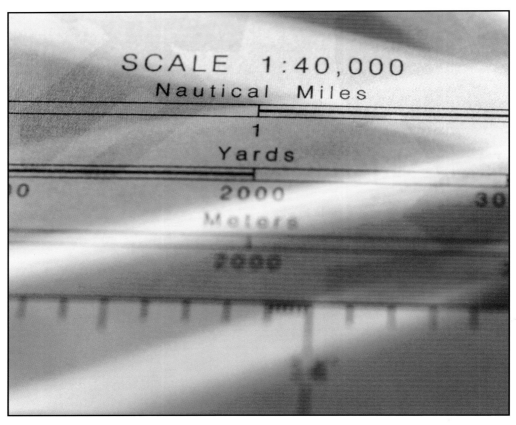

The scale on this map uses the ratio 1:40,000. This means that distances on the map are 1/40,000 their actual length. This particular scale allows a person to measure distances in nautical miles, yards, and meters.

Knowing an object's perimeter has many practical uses. If you want to fence in a backyard, measuring the yard's perimeter will tell you how much fencing you need to buy. If you are decorating the walls in your home and want to put up a wallpaper border, you would need to know the rooms' perimeters. Simply add the lengths of all the walls and you will know how long the border must be.

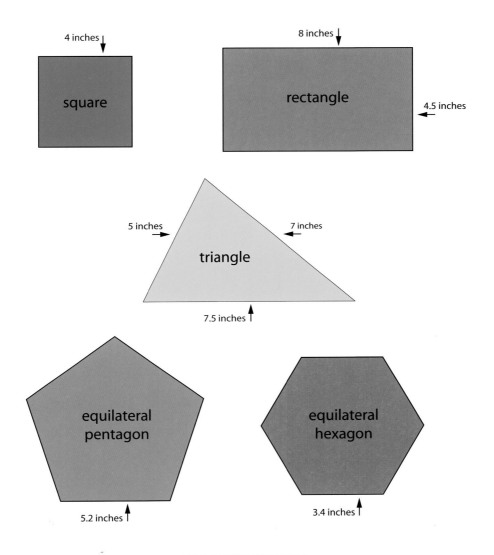

4 inches

square

8 inches

rectangle

4.5 inches

5 inches

triangle

7 inches

7.5 inches

equilateral
pentagon

equilateral
hexagon

5.2 inches

3.4 inches

MEASUREMENTS NOT TO SCALE

Look at the shapes above. Can you calculate their perimeters? Answers appear on page 42.

CIRCUMFERENCE

How do you measure a round object like a circle? Scientists from the past thought about this question and performed experiments to answer it. A length of a line that is drawn around a sphere or ball would give the ball's circumference. This line is in the shape of a circle. (This is only true for spheres and circles.) How do you measure the length of the line? If the ball is small enough, you might be able to use a tape measure. But what if the ball is too large for you to use a measuring tool? You would need to use an equation that would help you calculate the circumference of the circle.

The circumference of a circle always has the same ratio to the circle's **diameter.** The diameter is the straight line drawn from one side of the circle to the other. The line must pass through the center of the circle. (The **radius** is the length from the center of the circle to the edge of the circle. It is half of the diameter.) This ratio of circumference to diameter is the same for all circles—no matter what size they may be. This constant is called **pi.** (It is written with the Greek letter π, and pronounced like *pie*.) The value of pi is approximately 22/7 or 3.14. This means that any circle's circumference is a little bit more than three times the length of the diameter.

An equation was developed to calculate circumference. It uses diameter—or radius—and pi. In order to use it you will need to know either the diameter or radius of the circle. If you know the diameter you can use this equation (**d**= diameter):

d × π = **Circumference**

or

dπ = Circumference

If you only have the circle's radius you can use a different equation. The equation multiplies the radius by 2 since the radius is half of the diameter (**r** = radius):

2 × **r** × π = **Circumference**

or

2rπ = Circumference

For example, if the radius of a circle is 4 inches, you would fill in the equation like this 2 × 4 × π = Circumference. Substitute 3.14 for π and you get 2 × 4 × 3.14 = 25.12. So the circumference of the circle is 25.12 inches. What is the circumference of a circle with a diameter of 7 inches? How about a circle with a radius of 1.5 inches? (Answers appear on page 42.)

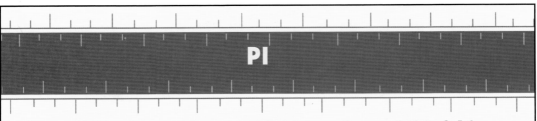

PI

The numeric value used to represent pi is usually rounded to 3.14. But pi's actual numeric value has an infinite number of decimal places. This means that the numbers following the decimal point go on forever. Computers have figured out pi's numeric value with many decimal places. Here is an example of pi with fifteen digits after the decimal point:

3.141592653589793

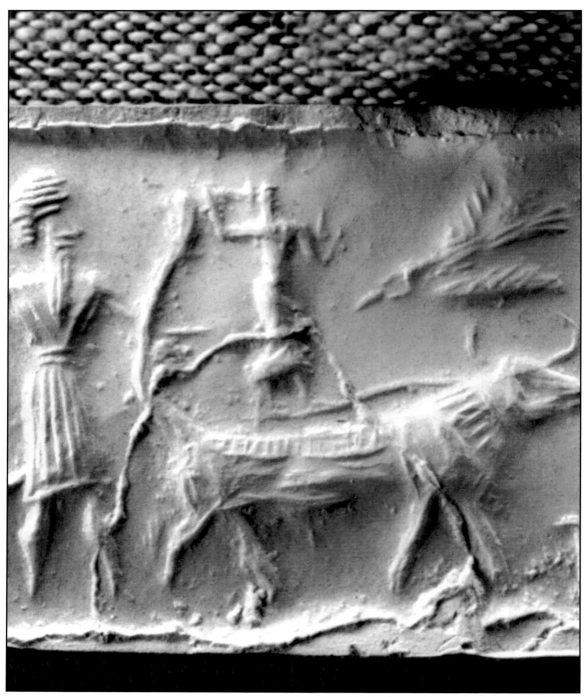

An artifact from Mesopotamia—around 2350 BCE—shows a farmer and his ox working a field. In ancient times, working the land was one of the only ways to measure distance and area.

CHAPTER FOUR

Measuring Area

Five thousand years ago, in Ancient Mesopotamia—which included parts of present-day Middle Eastern countries—people did not use mathematics to calculate area. They did not have formulas or equations. They defined a piece of land by working on it. They asked questions like *How many narrow strips were being cultivated or used for crops?* Later, this became *What could be plowed with two oxen in a day?* (This amount actually works out to be about the same as the **acre** we use today.) But it was not easy to measure land this way. Not only was it hard physical work, but you also had to bring a team of oxen with you! Fortunately, early mathematicians eventually developed units and equations.

SQUARES AND RECTANGLES

To measure the area of squares and rectangles, you multiply the width by the length. The simple equation is this:

Length x Width = Area measured in square units

In squares, all sides are the same. So multiplying a square's width by its length is the same as multiplying the number by itself. When you do this, it is called squaring a number. So multiplying 3 by 3 is the same

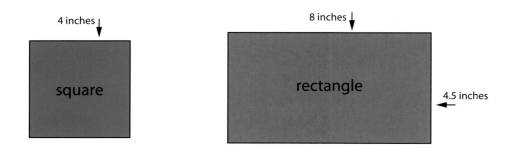

4 inches

square

8 inches

rectangle

4.5 inches

Can you calculate the area of these two shapes? Answers appear on page 42.

as squaring the number 3. Squaring a number can also be written as n^2, in which *n* represents any number. So 3 squared is 3^2. Either way you write it, it still equals 9.

The units used to measure area are square versions of the units for length. A square foot is the area of a square with sides that measure 1 foot each (1 foot x 1 foot = 1 square foot or 1 ft^2). A square yard works the same way. It is the area of a square with sides that measure 1 yard each (1 yard x 1 yard = 1 square yard or 1 yd^2).

With a rectangle, not all the sides are equal. So multiplying width by length involves multiplying two different numbers. For example, the area of a rectangle with a length of 2 yards and a width of 1/2 yard is 1 square yard (2 yards x 1/2 yard = 1 square yard).

Once this concept was understood, the area of the land could be measured without oxen. Large pieces of land are often measured in

These plots of farmland are more or less rectangular, which makes it easier to figure out their areas.

acres. The acre is now defined as 4,840 square yards or 43,560 square feet.

Plots of land are often square or rectangular. But not every piece of land is exactly square or rectangular. How do you measure the area of those pieces of land? You can usually break the land up into large and small rectangles and squares. Add up their individual areas and you get the total land area.

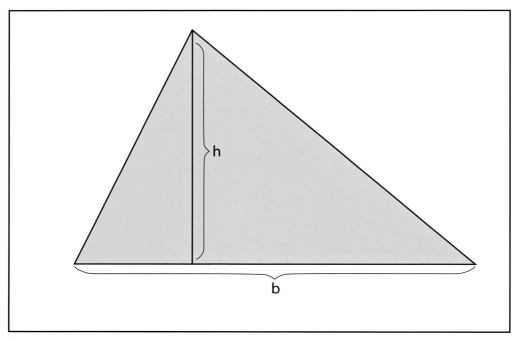

Calculating the area of most triangles requires knowing the measurement of the base (b) and the triangle's height (h).

TRIANGLES

When you break up a large irregularly shaped piece of land to calculate its area you might end up with rectangles, squares, and triangles. You can use the measurements of a triangle's sides to calculate its area. If **b** stands for the triangle's base and **h** is the height, you can use this formula to calculate area:

$$.5 \times b \times h = area$$

So if a triangle has a base that measure 5 inches and a height that is 8 inches, the area would be 20 square inches (.5 x 5 x 8 = 20).

UNITS OF AREA

Customary

1 square foot = 144 square inches
1 square yard = 9 square feet
1 acre = 4,840 square yards
1 square mile = 640 acres

Metric

1 square centimeter = 100 square millimeters
1 square meter = 1,000 square centimeters
1 hectare = 10,000 square meters
1 square kilometer = 100 hectares

CUSTOMARY CONVERSIONS

To convert customary units to metric units you can do the following:

To change	into	multiply by
square mile	square kilometer	2.59
acre	hectare	.40
square yard	square meter	.84
square foot	square meter	.09
square inch	square centimeter	6.45

METRIC CONVERSIONS

To convert metric units to customary units you can do the following:

To change	into	multiply by
square kilometer	square mile	.386
hectare	acre	2.47
square meter	square yard	1.19
square meter	square feet	10.76
square centimeter	square inch	1.55

CIRCLES

Sometimes you need to calculate circular areas. But a circle has no length or width. So how can you measure its area? As with circumference, you will use the radius (or diameter) and π. Picture a circle with the radius marked. Now imagine that the radius is going to move, sweeping around the circle like the hands of a clock. The radius of a circle is always the same, whether it is pointing to the top of the circle or the bottom. This is why the radius is useful in calculating a circle's area.

Using r to represent the radius, the equation for a circle's area is

$$\pi \times r^2 = \textbf{Area}$$

or

$$\pi \, r^2 = \textbf{Area}$$

So if you had a circle with a radius of 4 inches, the area would be 50.24 ($\pi \times 4^2$ or π x 4 x 4). What is the area of a circle with a radius of 3.5 inches? How about a circle with a diameter of 16 inches? (Answers appear on pages 42 and 43.)

SURFACE AREA

You can use your knowledge of measuring area to calculate the surface area of some objects. The surface area is the total area of all sides of a three-dimensional object. Cubes and boxes are three-dimensional squares or rectangles. To measure surface area, first calculate the area of all the sides. Add the totals together and you get the surface area. So if you had a cube with sides that were 6 inches long you would have a surface are a of 216 square inches. This is because each side of the cube is a square with sides that measure 6 inches each. So the area of one of those squares is 36 inches. A cube has 6 sides, so you need to multiply the area by 6. (6^2 x 6 = 216).

The equation used to calculate a cylinder's surface area has two parts: the area of the circular top and bottom added to the area of the sides. The area of each of the circles at the top and bottom of the cylinder is $πr^2$. There are two circles so you would multiply the area by 2, giving you **2 x $πr^2$** or **$2πr^2$**

The second part of the equation is the area of the cylinder's sides. Think of the cylinder's sides as a rolled-up rectangle. To find the area of that rectangle you would multiply the height (h) by the length. The length of the rectangle is the circle's circumference (**$2πr$**). So the area of that rectangle is **$2πr$ x h** or **$2πrh$**. Adding those two parts together, you get the equation for the total surface area of a cylinder:

$$2πr^2 + 2πrh = \textbf{surface area of a cylinder}$$

It is even harder to physically measure the surface area of a sphere, so you must use the simple equation:

$$4πr^2 = \textbf{surface area of a sphere}$$

Measuring surface area has practical uses. If you are wrapping a gift, but running low on wrapping paper, you might want to know if you will have enough paper. You can figure this out by calculating the surface area of the gift. Then measure the area of your sheets of wrapping paper.

Graduated cylinders, flasks, and beakers are used to measure liquid volumes.

CHAPTER FIVE

Measuring Volume

Volume is the amount of space a three-dimensional object takes up. In earlier times, volume was not measured with equations. For example, some cultures figured out volume by using weight. The capacity (volume) of a jar was equal to the total weight of the dry seeds that filled the jar. In medieval England, a gallon was defined as 8 pounds of wheat. Today, however, we use formulas and units of length to measure volume.

An object's volume is its length times its width times its height:

Length x Width x Height = Volume

So a cube with 1-inch sides has a volume of 1 cubic inch (1 inch x 1 inch x 1 inch = 3 cubic inches or 3 in^3.) What is the volume of a rectangular box with a length of 10 inches, a width of 4 inches, and a height of 5 inches? (Answer is on page 43.)

Using the customary system, volumes of solids can be measured in units of cubic feet, cubic inches, or cubic yards. In the metric system, units would include cubic centimeters or cubic meters.

Liquids also have volumes. Fluid volume is usually measured using marked containers such as measuring cups or graduated cylinders. The units used to describe these measurements include fluid ounces, cups, pints, quarts, and gallons. Metric measurements include milliliters and liters. Interestingly, the volume of a fluid can also be shown in cubic centimeters.

These seven liquid measuring containers were made in the 1850s. Each represented a standard liquid volume.

VOLUME OF A SPHERE

How would you calculate the volume of a sphere? Again, you would use the diameter, radius, and π. The formula for the volume of a sphere involves cubing the radius. Cubing a number means multiplying it by itself three times. So cubing the number 2 is the same as 2 x 2 x 2. It can also be written as 2^3. The answer is 8. The formula for calculating the volume of a sphere is

4/3 x π x r^3 = Volume in cubic units

or

4/3 π r^3 = Volume

A sphere with a radius of 3 inches has a volume of 113.04 cubic inches (4/3 x 3.14 x 3^3 = 113.04). What is the volume of a sphere with a diameter of 8 inches? (Answer appears on page 43.)

DISPLACEMENT

There is another way to measure the volume of a solid without using these formulas. Placing an object into a container of liquid—such as water—will make the water rise. The object is displacing a specific amount of water. Measuring the amount of water displaced will give you the volume of the solid object. For example, a small rock that displaces 4 cubic centimeters of water has a volume of 4 cubic centimeters.

The water level on the glass at left is marked with blue tape. After a plastic container is dropped into the glass, the water level rises above the blue tape. The amount of water being displaced is the volume of the plastic object.

UNITS OF VOLUME

Customary

8 ounces = 1 cup

1 pint = 2 cups

1 quart = 2 pints or 4 cups

1 gallon = 4 quarts

1 cubic yard = 27 cubic feet

1 cubic foot = 1,728 cubic inches

Metric

1 milliliter = 1/1,000 liter

1 cubic centimeter = 1 milliliter

1 cubic centimeter = 1,000
cubic millimeters

CUSTOMARY CONVERSIONS

To convert customary units to metric units you can do the following:

To change	into	multiply by
cups	milliliters	236.59
gallons	liters	3.79
cubic yard	cubic meter	.764
cubic foot	cubic meter	.028

METRIC CONVERSIONS

To convert metric units to customary units you can do the following:

To change	into	divide by
milliliters	cups	236.59
liters	gallons	3.79
cubic meter	cubic yard	.764
cubic meter	cubic foot	.028

EXPERIMENT

You will need a measuring cup, tap water, and assorted pebbles. Fill the container half-full of water. Note the level of the water using the marks on the side. Now gently place one pebble in the cup and check the water level. The difference between the first measurement and the second is the volume of the pebble. Try out the other pebbles—one at a time—and find out how they differ in volume.

From the beginning of human history, people have tried to answer a simple question: How big is it? They have attempted to measure everything around them—the area of a piece of farmland, the distance to a faraway star, the volume of water in a glass. They have used tools as basic as their own bodies, and technologies as advanced as instruments that measure waves of light. And these efforts to determine area, distance, and volume are every bit as important today as they were thousands of years ago—because measuring our surroundings is an essential part of understanding them.

GLOSSARY

acre—A customary unit of area. It is equal to 43,560 square feet. In metric measurements it is equal to 4,046.86 square meters or 0.4 hectare.

area—A measurement that represents the size of a specific space.

caliper—A tool used to measure an object's thickness.

circumference—The distance around the outside of a circle or sphere.

diameter—The length of a straight line drawn from one side of the circle to the other side. This line must pass through the circle's center.

displacement—When an object takes the place of another. Used as a method for determining an object's volume.

micron—1/1000 millimeter. It is also called a micrometer.

perimeter—The distance around an object's borders.

pi—The constant ratio of a circle's diameter to its circumference. It is represented by the Greek letter π.

radius—The distance from the center of a circle to its outer edge.

stade—A measurement used by Ancient Romans to represent 100 paces of a marching man.

surface area—The total area of all surfaces of a three-dimensional object.

FIND OUT MORE

BOOKS

Gardner, Robert. *Far-out Science Projects with Height and Depth: How High Is Up? How Low Is Down?* Berkeley Heights, NJ: Enslow Publishers, 2003.

Richards, John. *Units & Measurements*. Brookfield, CT: Copper Beech Books, 2000.

Woodford, Chris. *Area*. San Diego, CA: Blackbirch Press, 2005.

WEB SITES

Measurement Resources
http://mathforum.org/paths/measurement/m.measlessons.html

Understanding the Area of a Circle
http://www.wku.edu/~tom.richmond/Pir2.html

CALCULATING HEIGHT USING RATIOS

For very tall objects, such as buildings or trees, you cannot use a tape measure or ruler to measure height directly. However, by using shadows and ratios you can gain an idea—though not necessarily an exact measurement—of how tall the building or tree may be.

Materials:

A straight stick around 2 feet long
A tape measure

Instructions:

You need to do this experiment on a sunny day. Push the stick into the ground, making sure that it is standing straight up. (If you are working on a paved area, you can use an empty bottle or jar filled with sand to hold the stick upright.) Measure the height of the stick, from the ground to the top of the stick. (Do not include the part that is buried.) Measure the length of the shadow of the stick.

Figure out how the length of the shadow is related to the length of the stick. For example, if the shadow's length is 1 inch and the stick is 10 inches, you know that the shadow is one-tenth of the height of the stick. (1 inch x 10 = 10 inches so 1/10 of 10 inches is 1 inch.) This can be expressed in a ratio of 1:10. If the length of the shadow is 3 inches and the stick is 12 inches, then you know that the shadow is one-fourth of the length of the stick. (3 inches x 4 = 12 inches.) The ratio for this is 1:4.

Pick out a tall tree or building and measure its shadow. You must make sure to measure the shadow on the same day and at nearly the same time as when you measured the stick's shadow. This ensures that the sun has not moved, altering the shadow's lengths.

If you know the ratio of the stick's height to the stick's shadow, you can figure out the approximate height of the tree or building. For example, the ratio for the shadow's length to the stick's height is 1:4—this means that the stick is four times longer than the shadow. Using this ratio, if the tree's shadow is 10 feet long, approximately how tall is the tree?

(Answer appears on page 43.)

Chapter 3
Page 21, (perimeters):
Square: 16 inches
Rectangle: 25 inches
Triangle: 19.5 inches
Hexagon: 20.4 inches
Pentagon: 26 inches

Page 23, (circumference of a circle):
Note: π = 3.14
A circle with a diameter of 7 inches will have a circumference of 21.98 inches (7 x π = 21.98).

A circle with a radius of 1.5 inches will have a circumference of 9.42 inches (2 x 1.5 x π = 9.42).

Chapter 4
Page 26 (area of a square and rectangle):
Square: 16 square inches
Rectangle: 36 square inches

Page 30 (area of a circle):
Note: π = 3.14
A circle with a radius of 3.5 inches will have an area of 38.465 square inches (π x 3.5^2 = 38. 465 square inches).

A circle with a diameter of 16 inches will have an area of 200.96 square inches. Remember, the formula uses the radius, which is half of the diameter. So first you must change the diameter into a radius (16/2 = 8). So π x 8^2 = 200.96 square inches

Chapter 5

Page 33 (volume of a rectangular box):
The answer is 200 cubic inches. The measurements of the box are 10 inches (length), 4 inches (width), and 5 inches (height) so you would use this equation:

10 x 4 x 5 = 200 cubic inches

Page 33 (volume of a sphere):
The answer is 267.95 cubic inches. Remember, the formula uses the radius, which is half of the diameter. So first you must change the diameter into a radius (8/2 = 4)
4/3 x π x 4^3 = 267.95 cubic inches

Page 40 (calculating height using ratios):
The answer is 40 feet. If the ratio from the shadow to the stick is 1:4, then the ratio from the tree's shadow to the tree is also 1:4. So the tree must be 4 times taller than the shadow. The shadow is 10 feet long, so you multiply it by 4 and get 40 feet (10 x 4 = 40).

INDEX

ABOUT THE AUTHOR

Navin Sullivan has an M.A. in science from the University of Cambridge. He lives with his wife in London, England, and has dedicated many years to science education. He has edited various science texts, and has written science books for younger readers. Navin Sullivan has also been the CEO of a British educational publisher and Chairman of its Boston subsidiary. His hobbies include playing the piano and chess.